Dear Parent:

Congratulations! Your child is taking the first steps on an exciting journey. The destination? Independent reading!

STEP INTO READING® will help your child get there. The program offers books at five levels that accompany children from their first attempts at reading to reading success. Each step includes fun stories, fiction and nonfiction, and colorful art. There are also Step into Reading Sticker Books, Step into Reading Math Readers, and Step into Reading Phonics Readers— a complete literacy program with something to interest every child.

Learning to Read, Step by Step!

Ready to Read Preschool–Kindergarten
• big type and easy words • rhyme and rhythm • picture clues
For children who know the alphabet and are eager to begin reading.

Reading with Help Preschool–Grade 1
• basic vocabulary • short sentences • simple stories
For children who recognize familiar words and sound out new words with help.

Reading on Your Own Grades 1–3
• engaging characters • easy-to-follow plots • popular topics
For children who are ready to read on their own.

Reading Paragraphs Grades 2–3
• challenging vocabulary • short paragraphs • exciting stories
For newly independent readers who read simple sentences with confidence.

Ready for Chapters Grades 2–4
• chapters • longer paragraphs • full-color art
For children who want to take the plunge into chapter books but still like colorful pictures.

STEP INTO READING® is designed to give every child a successful reading experience. The grade levels are only guides. Children can progress through the steps at their own speed, developing confidence in their reading, no matter what their grade.

Remember, a lifetime love of reading starts with a single step!

*For my brother Michael, charmed by cars,
and for Shana Corey, charming editor
—M.K.*

*For two of the most interesting and likable
people I know—my brothers, Bill and John
—R.W.*

*With special thanks to Mark Patrick, Curator of the National Automotive History
Collection of the Detroit Public Library, for his time and expertise in reviewing this book.*

Photo credit (page 48): From the Collections of Henry Ford Museum & Greenfield Village.

www.stepintoreading.com

Educators and librarians, for a variety of teaching tools, visit us at
www.randomhouse.com/teachers

Library of Congress Cataloging-in-Publication Data
Kulling, Monica.
Eat my dust! : Henry Ford's first race / by Monica Kulling ; illustrated by Richard Walz.
    p.   cm. — (Step into reading. A step 3 book)
SUMMARY: Relates the excitement caused by Henry Ford as he drove the "horseless carriage"
he built, particularly when he decided to win a race to get money to build a new car that
anyone could afford.
ISBN 0-375-81510-4 (trade) — ISBN 0-375-91510-9 (lib. bdg.)
1. Ford, Henry, 1863–1947—Juvenile literature. 2. Automobile engineers—United States—
Biography—Juvenile literature. 3. Automobiles, Racing—Juvenile literature. [1. Ford, Henry,
1863–1947. 2. Automobile racing—History. 3. Automobiles, Racing. 4. Industrialists.
5. Automobile industry and trade—Biography.]
I. Title. II. Series: Step into reading. Step 3 book.
TL140.F6K85   2004   338.7'6292'092—dc21   2003001190

Printed in the United States of America   First Edition   10 9 8 7 6 5 4 3 2 1

Eat My Dust!
Henry Ford's First Race

by Monica Kulling
illustrated by Richard Walz

Random House 🏠 New York

Henry Ford liked to drive.

He liked to drive into town.

People got excited

when they saw him.

"There is that crazy Henry
driving his horseless buggy
again," they said.

Ladies ran for the sidewalk.

Men leaped for cover.

Dogs barked.

Horses reared.

Henry liked driving into town.

Henry had built

his car by himself.

It ran on gas.

It did not have brakes.

Henry stopped his car

by turning off the engine.

Then he jumped out.

Henry tied his car to a post—

just like a horse—

so it would not roll away.

Everyone wished
Henry would go back
to driving a horse and buggy.
But Henry loved cars.
He loved driving them.
And he loved building them.

Other people were
building cars, too.
Their cars cost a lot of money.
They always needed repairs.
Since most people
did not know how to drive,
car owners hired drivers.
Only the rich
could afford to own a car.

Henry had a dream.

He wanted to build a car

everyone could own.

Henry needed money

to build his dream car.

How could he get it?

He decided to enter a race.

Henry had never

raced a car in his life!

Car racing was a new sport.
People dressed up
for a day at the races.
They cheered the fastest car
to victory.

"If I win the race,"
Henry told his wife, Clara,
"I will be able to build
my new car."

Henry and a mechanic
named Spider Huff
went to work.
They put a twenty-six-
horsepower engine
in their race car.
One horsepower equaled
the pulling power
of one horse.
That meant Henry's car
could beat any horse—
in seconds flat!

People laughed
at Henry.
"You'll never beat
the Daredevil!"
they said.
The Daredevil
was Alexander Winton.
He was the American
racing car champion.

"I can beat him," said Henry.

"My car is built better."

Clara nodded.

She wanted only one thing.

She wanted Henry

to drive safely.

The races were held at a track
near Detroit, Michigan.
Henry entered
the ten-mile race.
The prize was $1,000.
Eight thousand people
filled the stands that day.

The ten-mile race
was the last race of the day.
Henry and Winton
were the only racers
on the track.
The Daredevil
smiled at Henry.
He tipped his hat.
Henry tipped his hat
and smiled back.

"On your marks!"

shouted the starter.

Henry gripped

the steering wheel.

"Start your engines!"

Spider cranked the engine.

Henry's racer roared to life.

Bang!

The starter's pistol went off.

Henry and Winton

shot down the track!

The crowd cheered.
Most were cheering
for Winton.
They were sure
he would win.

The two cars
raced side by side.
Up ahead lay the first curve.
Winton was a pro.
He knew how to drive
around a bend
without slowing down.
Henry did not.
He had to cut the engine.
Then he made
a slow, wide turn.

"Lean out!"

shouted Henry.

Spider stood

on the running board.

He leaned out.

Henry took the curve.

Spider's weight

kept the racer

from tipping over.

Winton was ahead.
Henry stepped on the gas.
He sped down the track.
His car caught up
with Winton's.
The cars raced
around the track
five more times.

The racers were

on their last lap.

The finish line was in sight.

Suddenly black smoke

covered the track.

Henry could not see.

Was his car in trouble?

Was the engine overheating?

Was the race to build

his dream car over?

No.

Winton's car

was in trouble.

It was burning oil.

Suddenly

the engine stalled.

Winton's car rolled to a stop.

Henry roared past

in a cloud of dust!

"Yippee!"

he shouted with glee.

The crowd went wild.

Men threw their hats

in the air.

Women stood on their chairs

to get a better view.

Henry had won

his first car race!

Henry Ford was the new

American racing car champion!

The next day,

Henry's name and picture

were in all the newspapers.

He had won the money.

He had also won a beautiful
crystal punch bowl.
Clara placed the bowl
on the table
for visitors to see.

Henry built his dream car.

He called it the Model T.

It came in one color—black.

The Model T

was easy to drive.

It was easy to repair.

People loved it.

They called it

the Tin Lizzie.

Henry Ford drove
his Tin Lizzie into town.
People got excited
when they saw him.
Ladies waved.
Men honked.
Henry was happy.
He had built a car
everyone could own.

AUTHOR'S NOTE

This is a true story.

The race was held

on October 10, 1901.

Henry used the prize money

to build the Ford Motor Company.

Henry Ford's Model T

was a car everyone could own.

And almost everyone did.

This is a photo of the actual race. Henry is just about to pass Winton. If you look closely, you can see Spider on the running board!